Discovering Mission San Miguel Arcángel

BY JACK CONNELLY

Cavendish Square

New York

Published in 2015 by Cavendish Square Publishing, LLC
243 5th Avenue, Suite 136, New York, NY 10016

Copyright © 2015 by Cavendish Square Publishing, LLC

First Edition

Website: cavendishsq.com

This publication represents the opinions and views of the author based on his or her personal experience, knowledge, and research. The information in this book serves as a general guide only. The author and publisher have used their best efforts in preparing this book and disclaim liability rising directly or indirectly from the use and application of this book.

CPSIA Compliance Information: Batch #WS14CSQ

All websites were available and accurate when this book was sent to press.

Library of Congress Cataloging-in-Publication Data

Connelly, Jack.
Discovering Mission San Miguel Arcángel / Jack Connelly.
pages cm. — (California missions)
Includes index.
ISBN 978-1-62713-088-2 (hardcover) ISBN 978-1-62713-090-5 (ebook)
1. Mission San Miguel Arcangel (San Miguel, Calif.)—History—Juvenile literature. 2. Spanish mission buildings—California—San Miguel—History—Juvenile literature. 3. Franciscans—California—San Miguel—History—Juvenile literature. 4. Salinan Indians—Missions—California—San Miguel—History—Juvenile literature. 5. California—History—To 1846—Juvenile literature. I. Edgar, Nancy A. II. Title.
F869.M666E34 2015
979.4'63—dc23
2014006018

Editorial Director: Dean Miller
Editor: Kristen Susienka
Copy Editor: Cynthia Roby
Art Director: Jeffrey Talbot
Designer: Douglas Brooks
Photo Researcher: J8 Media
Production Manager: Jennifer Ryder-Talbot
Production Editor: David McNamara

Printed in the United States of America

Contents

Mission San Miguel Arcángel is one of the missions that shaped California's early history in the late 1700s and 1800s.

1
The Spanish Explore California

At the edge of the town of San Miguel, California, Mission San Miguel Arcángel stands as a reminder of Spanish efforts to colonize the land. In 1797, it became the sixteenth in a chain of twenty-one missions along the California coast founded by Spanish **friars** (*frays* in Spanish) between 1769 and 1823.

SPAIN LEARNS ABOUT THE NEW WORLD

Spain's interest in California began after explorer Christopher Columbus brought back news of the lands he called the New World, or the Americas. Although many people had lived on these lands for thousands of years, the Americas were unknown to Europeans until this time. The Spanish were eager to explore these lands and claim them for themselves. They wanted to make their empire larger and hoped to find gold, spices, and other riches.

CREATING A NEW SPAIN

In order to take command of land in America without sending a large number of settlers, the Spanish government decided to turn the people already living there into Spanish citizens. They would do this by teaching the **indigenous people** the Spanish language, customs, and religious beliefs. In 1519, Hernán Cortés went to the area that today is Mexico and conquered the Aztec empire. The Spanish claimed this land and called it New Spain.

BAJA AND ALTA CALIFORNIA

King Carlos III sent soldiers and friars to start missions in Alta California.

After the Spanish claimed New Spain, they became interested in some of the land to the north. This land is now California and the part of Mexico that is called the Baja Peninsula. The state of California was then called *Alta*, or "upper," California, while the Baja Peninsula was known as *Baja*, or "lower," California.

The explorer Juan Rodríguez Cabrillo sailed to Alta California in 1542, where he found what was later called San Diego Bay. In 1602, another explorer, Sebastián Vizcaíno, traveled to Alta California. He sailed around what is now Monterey Bay. Since neither Cabrillo nor Vizcaíno found gold or rich nations to conquer, the Spanish did not think it was worth the time and money necessary to colonize Alta California.

It wasn't until 1769 that the Spanish sent soldiers and missionaries to begin the Alta California missions. The Spanish king, Carlos III, feared that colonists from Russia and Britain would take over these lands. To prevent this, he ordered the government in New Spain to establish missions in Alta California as quickly as possible.

2 The Salinan

When the Spanish settlers came to Alta California, they found the land already populated by close to 300,000 Native Californians. These Natives were members of different groups of people, known as tribes, and each one had its own customs and language. Most of the Natives living in the San Miguel region were part of the Salinan people, with a small number of Chumash too. It is difficult to learn the origins of the Salinan, as they did not leave a written record of their history. Scientists known as archeologists carefully dig up the sites of past villages in order to unearth clues about the Salinan way of life and to piece together how these Natives used to live.

Many Native tribes, including the Salinan, made dome-shaped houses from branches and brush around them.

HUNTER-GATHERERS

The lifestyle of the Salinan —their homes, diet, work, and religion— were all linked to nature. Much of the Salinan's daily life was spent searching for plants, animals, fish, and insects. The Salinan women, who did most of the gathering, collected the roots, seeds, berries, and nuts that were the staples of their diet.

Acorns were an important source of nutrition for the Salinan, and were used in soups, cakes, and breads. However, acorns have a bitter acid that makes them taste very bad. The Salinan women developed a special way to prepare them to make them more appetizing. First, they ground the acorns into raw flour by crushing them between two rocks, called a mortar and pestle. Then they placed the acorn flour in a sandy pit or a basket and poured hot water over it to wash away the bitterness. This had to be done many times to ensure the acorn flour was ready to eat.

The Salinan men hunted with spears, bows, and arrows. Their

Many Native people lived in villages. Everyone worked together to survive. Men often hunted while women cooked and gathered acorns and other vegetation to eat.

arrowheads and spear tips were made of rocks chipped to form a hard point that could pierce an animal's skin. Strong, flexible tree branches were used to make their bows. They made bowstrings from vegetable stalks or animal tendons, called sinews.

VILLAGES

The Salinan built their homes using materials that grew in the area. They used local wood to make a cone-shaped frame, and then tied layers of brush and tule grass thatching to it. The thatch worked like shingles to keep the rain out.

The Salinan lived in villages of thirty to 300 people. Since they lived off the land, they had to move during the different times of the year when water or food in the area became scarce. They also moved when their homes became old, weathered, or unstable. In the fall, the Salinan moved to temporary shelters near forests of oak trees in order to harvest as many acorns as possible.

CLOTHING

Throughout much of the year, the Salinan men wore little or no clothing. The women wore skirts made out of bark, grass, or animal hides. In cooler weather, everyone draped hides over their shoulders for warmth. The Salinan wore necklaces and earrings made of abalone shells. Both men and women wore their hair long.

A WAY OF LIFE

The Salinan believed many spirits were at work in nature. They believed that medicine men, or shamans, were able to cure illnesses. The shamans treated the sick by dancing, singing, and using herbal medicines.

In addition to fighting off illness, Salinan people used singing and dancing in many other ceremonies, including ones tied to births, marriages, deaths, and when young men and women became adults. To further honor these occasions, the Salinan would also paint their bodies sometimes.

Each year many acorns were gathered and stored for later use.

3
The
Mission System

While the Spanish government wanted to build missions to create more Spanish citizens and claim land for Spain, the friars were eager to teach Native Californians about **Christianity**. They believed that only Christians would go to heaven after they died, and they wanted to save the souls of the indigenous people.

Soldiers were sent to help with the building of the mission complex, to watch over the people at the mission, and to protect the complex against Native people who didn't want the Spanish on their lands. Each mission had four or five soldiers who lived in the complex. In some areas, the Spanish built forts, called *presidios*, to protect the missions from attack.

CULTURAL MISUNDERSTANDINGS

The Salinan lived very differently than the European missionaries, who regarded them as people who were "uncivilized," or as children who needed to be taught to live "properly." The Spanish perceived the Salinan as inferior because they were not educated in schools, they lived in temporary homes, and they worshipped many spirits instead of the Christian god. The friars believed that teaching the Salinan how to live like Spaniards was in their best

Before Spanish intervention, the Salinan had established their own beliefs and traditions. The Salinan, Chumash, and Yokut were all known for creating pictographs, such as this one at Painted Rock.

interest, and wanted to teach them how to farm, speak the Spanish language, and follow the Christian religion. They didn't realize, or acknowledge, that the Salinan led productive lives on their own.

When Native Californians joined a mission and **converted** to Christianity, they were called **neophytes**. Neophytes had to live at the mission and were not allowed to leave. The friars feared that if the neophytes left the mission, they might never return.

The Spanish hoped to train the neophytes in the Spanish way of life in ten years. After this period of time, the friars planned to turn the mission lands over to the neophytes. The neophytes would operate the mission as Spanish citizens and pay taxes to the Spanish government. The land itself would remain under the control of New Spain.

Once the Natives were ready to run the missions themselves, the Spanish originally planned to return the lands to them. However, this never happened, as settlers from Europe, Mexico, and other parts of America kept the land.

Over the years, twenty-one missions and four presidios were built along California's coast.

4
Founding the Mission

Once King Carlos III declared that missions should be set up in California, the government in New Spain sent five groups to Alta California under the military command of Captain Gaspár de Portolá. A **Franciscan** friar named Fray Junípero Serra was chosen as the president of the mission system in Alta California. He accompanied one of these groups.

THE SPANISH SETTLE ALTA CALIFORNIA

The expedition included soldiers, missionaries, and indigenous people who had converted to Christianity at missions in New Spain. Three ships, the *San Carlos*, the *San Antonio*, and the *San José*, sailed up the coast with the items the friars would need to begin the missions, including food supplies and religious articles such as crosses, statues, and robes. Other supplies were loaded on the backs of the pack mules that made the overland journey. Two groups traveled over the desert land of New Spain, herding cattle to Alta California.

All five groups were to meet near San Diego Bay at the beginning of July 1769. The journey was difficult, and many men became sick. The *San José* and its crew were lost at sea. More than half of the 219 sailors who started the journey to Alta California died.

Despite these hardships, the surviving settlers met in San Diego, and on July 16, 1769, Fray Serra founded Mission San Diego de Alcalá, the first mission in Alta California.

A NEED FOR A NEW MISSION

Mission San Miguel Arcángel was founded twenty-eight years after Fray Serra founded the first mission in Alta California. At this point Fray Serra had died, and a new mission president,

Fray Junípero Serra was the first president of the Alta California missions.

Fray Fermín Francisco Lasuén, was in charge. In 1795, the governor of California, Diego de Borica, decided that there was too large a gap between Mission San Luis Obispo de Tolosa and Mission San Antonio de Padua. It was more than a day's journey, and the Spanish did not like to travel at night. Governor Borica sent an expedition to find a suitable site for a new mission. Fray Buenaventura Sitjar of Mission San Antonio de Padua and a few soldiers formed this expedition.

Fray Sitjar wrote to Fray Lasuén that he had found a site near the Salinas River with the necessary sources of water and timber nearby. Located in a fertile valley with rich soil, the land was ideal for farming and ranching. It was also near a large Salinan village called Cholam. The Spanish hoped that many Salinan from this village would join the mission.

Governor Borica wrote to the **viceroy** of New Spain, Viceroy Marques de Branciforte, to ask for permission to build the mission and for 1,000 *pesos* for supplies. On August 19, 1796, Viceroy Branciforte wrote to say that the building could begin.

On July 25, 1797, Fray Lasuén founded Mission San Miguel Arcángel. Accompanied by Fray Sitjar and a few soldiers, Fray Lasuén blessed the spot, raised a cross, and performed a Christian church service called a Mass.

A WARM WELCOME

Unlike other settlements, the friars did not have much trouble getting the local people interested in the mission. Many of the Salinan who came to the founding had friends and relatives who lived at Mission San Antonio de Padua and at Mission San Luis Obispo de Tolosa. They wanted to learn more about the Spanish way of life. At the founding ceremony, the friars baptized fifteen Salinan children. **Baptism** is a ritual that is held when someone is accepted into the Christian religion. The missionaries were pleased that the Salinan wanted to join Mission San Miguel Arcángel.

The Spanish needed the Salinan's help to build the mission complex. Some of the Salinan wanted to try the Spanish tools, including their metal axes, which could chop down trees quickly. Other Salinan were attracted to the mission by gifts of food, beads, and fabrics offered by the Spanish in return for their work. In part because of the Salinan enthusiasm, building began right away.

THE MISSION'S EARLY BUILDINGS

After the founding ceremony, Fray Lasuén left the mission. Fray Sitjar was in charge, and Fray Antonio Horra assisted him. The missionaries, soldiers, and the Salinan at the mission built temporary shelters out of wooden planks and thatch, designed to last only until more permanent structures could be built.

After the shelters were built, the friars, soldiers, and neophytes began to make **adobe** bricks for more permanent buildings. The Spanish showed the Salinan how to mix mud, water, and straw to make adobe. The workers mixed the adobe with their feet and packed it into rectangular wooden molds. Once the bricks were molded, the workers placed them in the sun to dry. Mud was used to cement the bricks together to make walls. After the walls were completed, a roof was built of sticks and mud.

Guided by the friars and soldiers, men, women, and children worked together to create and operate the twenty-one missions.

5
The Mission Starts Strong

Fray Juan Francisco Martín joined the mission on December 3, 1797. A talented builder, he took the time to learn the Salinan language so that he could communicate with the neophytes he worked with at the mission.

SHAPING THE MISSION

After Fray Martín's arrival, work at Mission San Miguel Arcángel continued, and by the end of the month, three buildings were finished. In August 1799, Fray Sitjar left Mission San Miguel Arcángel to return to Mission San Antonio de Padua, and Fray Baltasar Carnicier came to Mission San Miguel Arcángel to assist Fray Martín. By December 31, 1800, five more adobe buildings were built. These included a dormitory, called a *monjerío*, for unmarried neophyte women and girls, a granary for storing grain, and a *convento*—a permanent adobe dwelling for the friars.

BUILDING AT MISSION SAN MIGUEL ARCÁNGEL

By 1804, hundreds of Salinan had come to live at the mission. Mission San Miguel Arcángel had all the spinning wheels, looms, and wool it needed for women to begin weaving blankets and cloth and making clothes. This became one of the principal industries at the mission. The neophytes were successfully raising livestock, and crops were planted and harvested in greater quantities than ever before.

The year 1805 was an important year for building. The neophytes constructed forty-seven houses for the neophyte village, called a *ranchería,* just outside the mission. As more buildings were added to the mission, they were placed in the shape of a quadrangle, or hollow square. In the center of the mission quadrangle was a courtyard. As the construction continued, the complex was expanded so that it eventually included the convento, monjerío, ranchería, dining rooms, kitchens, study rooms, workshops, granaries, stables, a corral, and a cemetery.

EXPANDING WITH RANCHOS

The mission grew so large that the friars established several *ranchos* for raising livestock. The ranchos usually had a chapel, stables, a corral, and housing for the neophytes. These were built miles from the main mission complex so the missionaries could work with the local people who lived in these areas. The ranchos at Mission San Miguel Arcángel included Rancho la Playa at San Simeón, Rancho de la Asunción, Rancho del Aguaje, Rancho el Paso de Robles, Rancho Santa Rosa, and Rancho Santa Ysabel.

The first rancho was begun in 1810, when a house and granary were built at Rancho la Playa. The rest of the ranchos were built between 1810 and 1820. There were hot springs at Rancho el Paso de Robles and Rancho de la Asunción that the friars and neophytes used during the cold, damp winters. The ranchos greatly added to Mission San Miguel Arcángel's ability to attract more neophytes.

ASKING FOR A NEW CHURCH

By 1814, Fray Martín and Fray Juan Cabot, who had come to replace Fray Carnicier, decided that there were so many neophytes at Mission San Miguel Arcángel that a new church was needed. They wrote to ask Governor José Argüello for a permit to build a larger church.

On December 14, 1814, Governor Argüello gave Fray Martín and Fray Cabot permission to build the first permanent church at the mission. The friars spent over a year planning and gathering the necessary materials. The neophytes made and stored adobe bricks. In 1816, the stone foundation for the new church was laid. Work continued steadily, and in 1819, the new church was finished.

PAINTING THE CHURCH

As the years went on, fewer Salinan were joining Mission San Miguel Arcángel, so new buildings did not need to be built. Fray Cabot asked a friend named Estéban Munras to come help the neophytes paint pictures on the walls inside the church. Munras helped design the bright and colorful **frescoes** inside the mission church. The artists at Mission San Miguel Arcángel had to make their own paints. To do this, they added linseed oil or cactus juice to dyes and pigments.

Munras wanted to paint designs that would make the inside of the church of Mission San Miguel Arcángel look like ancient

The neophytes who joined Mission San Miguel used their painting skills to decorate the church. Under instruction of painter Estebán Munras, some of the building's artwork was made to look like marble.

Roman buildings. Since the mission didn't have the materials to build detailed arches, balconies, and pillars, Munras and the neophytes painted them instead. The artists used a technique called marbleizing, which made objects look as if they were carved from marble. These paintings created the illusion that the arches and pillars were actually there.

In front of the church **sanctuary** is an altar. Behind the altar is the reredos—a large backboard with an eye painted on it to represent the all-seeing eye of God. Below are three statues: Saint Michael, Saint Anthony, and Saint Francis of Assisi. The friars used these objects when teaching the neophytes religious lessons.

6
Everyday Life

For the neophytes at Mission San Miguel Arcángel, their daily life was completely altered. They left their nomadic lifestyle behind, and no longer gathered plants or hunted. They had to learn how to farm, and make permanent houses. Christianity was new to them as well. As they learned more and more about the Spanish way of life, they left much of the Salinan culture behind.

ADJUSTING TO A NEW LIFE

Mission life was a difficult transition for many of the Salinan. For one thing, the neophytes were treated like children, and had to blindly obey the missionaries. They were not allowed to make their own decisions about what they wanted to do or wear, and were no longer allowed to worship the spirits of the Salinan religion. In addition to this lack of basic freedom, the neophytes were forced to follow a daily routine of work and prayer. While the friars at the missions were used to living lives that followed a strict schedule, the Salinan were not. Many neophytes had trouble adapting to the highly structured lifestyle of the friars.

A NEOPHYTE'S DAY

The mission bells woke the neophytes at dawn. Every morning they gathered for church services, followed by Bible lessons. After the services, the women served a breakfast of *atole*, a mush made of grain or corn. Next, the friars gave everyone his or her work assignment. The men labored in the fields, orchards, ranchos, and workshops, while the women cared for the small children and made food, baskets, cloth, and soap.

The Salinan men learned to grow corn, peas, beans, and barley. They also learned how to make charcoal, which was used for fuel and in paints. On the ranchos, they tended to the livestock, which included sheep, cattle, horses, mules, oxen, pigs, and goats. The Salinan men also worked in the mission's workshops to perfect their newly acquired skills in blacksmithing, carpentry, tanning, and making tiles and adobe bricks. When the mission needed repairs, the men worked with the friars to rebuild or refinish the buildings.

Friars taught neophytes trades such as weaving and farming.

To prepare the food for the residents of the mission, the Salinan women learned Spanish cooking techniques from the missionaries, who required them to use corn and wheat flour instead of acorn flour. They were taught to spin yarn out of the wool from the sheep raised at the mission. The friars showed them how to weave on looms so they could make blankets and European-style clothing. Mission San Miguel Arcángel actually became known for its wool, which was often traded with other missions in California for supplies.

The women also made soap by using ashes and fat from animals, called tallow.

During the day, neophyte children were taught by the friars about **Catholicism**. They also learned Spanish and Latin—Spanish was important for communicating with the new Spanish settlers, and Latin was important because at that time all Masses were conducted in Latin.

Neophytes would work all morning until about twelve. After the morning work session, the women served a lunch of *pozole*, a soup made of grain with a little meat and vegetables. Then it was time for a *siesta*, or rest. Work started back up in the afternoon around two o'clock, and continued until around five o'clock. Then it was time for Mass. After prayers, a simple dinner was served.

Finally, after a hard day of work and prayers, everyone was given a little time to relax. The Salinan liked to play games, sing,

and dance. A variety of games were played with sticks, hoops, and poles at the missions, many of which were from the Salinan culture. This free time was very limited, however, as the women went to bed at eight in the evening, and the men went to bed at nine.

HOLIDAYS AND FESTIVALS

Throughout the year, the people of the mission celebrated a number of holy days and other special occasions with *fiestas*. Many of these festivals honored Jesus Christ or other key saints. Sometimes the friars would blend older Salinan traditions with Catholic ceremonies in order to make the neophytes feel more involved with their new faith. Although the friars did not approve of these methods, they allowed them to try and keep the neophytes happy. The friars believed that if the Salinan were content, they'd be less likely to try and escape from the mission.

The land around Mission San Miguel Arcángel was used for farming and raising livestock.

7
Challenges at the Mission

In the first days of the mission, Fray Sitjar, Fray Horra, and the neophytes at Mission San Miguel Arcángel worked hard. They had few supplies, and there was much to be done. The missionaries and soldiers were far away from their homes and families, and they often felt isolated. The friars had to manage large farms and try to keep hundreds of neophytes happy with their life at the mission. Sometimes the stress was too much for friars who were put in charge.

EARLY PROBLEMS WITH FRAY HORRA

Fray Horra had trouble adjusting to mission life. Soon after he arrived at Mission San Miguel Arcángel, he wrote a letter to the viceroy in Mexico that read: "The treatment shown to the Indians is the most cruel I have ever read in history. For the slightest things they receive heavy flogging, and are shackled and put in the stocks, and treated with so much cruelty that they are kept whole days without water." This angered the other friars. If any friar inside the mission system criticized the treatment of the neophytes, trouble would soon follow. Thus the other friars at the mission isolated Fray Horra and declared him insane. About a month later,

Fray Horra was removed from Mission San Miguel Arcángel and escorted back to Spain under armed guard.

POSSIBLE POISONING?

After Fray Horra's departure, everything returned to normal and seemed to be going well at Mission San Miguel Arcángel until 1801, when Fray Martín and Fray Carnicier became sick. Fray Francisco Pujol came down from Mission San Antonio de Padua to help the two friars, and he became ill as well. Fray Martín and Fray Carnicier got better, but Fray Pujol died soon after returning to his own mission.

In light of this development, the friars accused some of the neophytes of poisoning them, and had the neophytes beaten for

Depicted in this late eighteenth-century etching by Henry Chapman Ford, Mission San Miguel Arcángel started to show disrepair over the years.

the crime. Later, evidence was discovered that the neophytes most probably had been wrongfully accused. It has been discovered that Fray Lasuén wrote in his journals that the true cause of the poisonings was a copper container lined with tin that held the friars' liquor. He believed that the container had become toxic, poisoning the drink.

A FIRE AND ITS EFFECTS

On August 25, 1806, a huge and devastating fire swept through Mission San Miguel Arcángel. The blaze destroyed two rows of buildings, the church roof, and more than 6,000 bushels of grain.

Restoration began soon after the fire. While many of the buildings were only in need of repairs, some had to be entirely rebuilt. At the same time, twenty-seven new homes for the neophytes were constructed in the ranchería.

One of the reasons that the fire had spread so quickly was

Mission San Miguel Arcángel suffered from a devastating fire in 1806 but was quickly rebuilt. Some buildings were redesigned to be more fire-resistant, with tile roofs as shown in this late nineteenth-century photograph.

because the original roofs were made of mud, sticks, and thatch. These materials caught fire easily, so the friars decided to rebuild the mission using tile roofs instead. They showed the neophytes how to make tiles from water and clay, which were much more fire resistant than the roofs that contained sticks and thatch.

A HARD LIFE FOR THE NEOPHYTES

Many of the Salinan at Mission San Miguel Arcángel resented their loss of freedom. Some neophytes had come to the mission only for the food and shelter it provided, and did not like being forced to obey the friars—or being punished if they failed to obey. To ease the tension at the mission, the friars allowed the neophytes to choose *alcaldes*, who served as police officers who communicated between the friars and the neophytes and tried to keep things peaceful. They also helped to oversee the neophytes' work, and punished those who were perceived as lazy or did not do their jobs well.

When neophytes tried to escape, soldiers and alcaldes were sent to bring them back. Runaways were beaten to discourage others from trying to leave. Another common punishment was locking neophytes in the stocks—wooden frames that had holes to hold a prisoner's wrists or ankles to keep him or her confined. At various missions throughout Alta California, the neophytes' treatment could be very brutal.

DISEASE

Sickness was common at all the missions, and caused many deaths. The neophytes were exposed to European diseases for the first time, including chicken pox, measles, and smallpox. While some of these illnesses didn't kill Europeans, they often proved deadly to the neophytes, whose bodies had not developed any resistance to them. Living quarters in the missions were often crowded and unsanitary as well, which increased the incidents of disease and death among the residents.

8
Secularization

The Spanish lost control of Mexico in 1821. Now that Mexico was an independent nation, it also gained control of the missions and surrounding land of Alta California.

MEXICO TAKES OVER THE MISSIONS

On January 6, 1831, the Mexican governor of California, Governor José María de Echeandia, issued a decree stating that the missions would soon be secularized. That day, four Mexican officials came to Mission San Miguel Arcángel to free the neophytes from the friars. One of the officials, José Castro, assembled the Salinan neophytes and told them that they were free to leave. The Salinan asked if they could consider the offer overnight. The next morning, most of the neophytes declined the offer, saying that they would be better off at the mission.

Red-tiled roofs were built to survive in the event of a fire.

In 1833, the Mexican government passed laws to secularize the missions. This meant that the neophytes would be free citizens of Spain. Unfortunately, while the government said that the neophytes were free from the rule of the

friars, it was now legal for the Mexican officials to force the neophytes to work the land that was taken from the Catholic Church. On August 9, 1834, the Mexican government seized Mission San Miguel Arcángel. The friars were allowed to stay and conduct church activities, but the government appointed Mexican officials to run the mission. These new officials were harsh with the Salinan, thus many left the mission. Some found jobs as cowboys, called *vaqueros*, or as servants on ranches in the area. Others tried to return to their old villages, but found that ranchers and settlers had taken their lands. Many Salinan had grown up at the mission and didn't know how to live off the land as their ancestors had.

After secularization, much of Mission San Miguel Arcángel fell into disrepair, but the church interior was kept in good condition.

CHANGE COMES TO THE MISSION

Under **secularization**, many mission lands that were supposed to be returned to the neophytes were sold or given away to settlers by Mexican officials. Two businessmen, Petronillo Ríos and William Reed, bought Mission San Miguel Arcángel in 1846.

The end of the mission system wasn't the only change in California during this time. When war broke out between the United States and Mexico, the American victors took possession of Alta California. Soon afterward, the California gold rush brought many people to the area, hoping to strike it rich. The area became the thirty-first state in 1850, and its name was shortened to California.

Although the mission faced many problems, it survives as a reminder of transformative times in California's early history.

9
Mission San Miguel Arcángel Today

United States president James Buchanan returned Mission San Miguel Arcángel to the Catholic Church in 1859, but the Church wouldn't send a new priest there for almost twenty years until Reverend Philip Farrelly arrived in 1878. He found many of the buildings had been rented out, and were now serving as living quarters, a store, a saloon, and a dance hall.

AFTERMATH OF SECULARIZATION

The town of San Miguel began to thrive after 1886, when railroad tracks connected it to Paso Robles and other towns in California. People found travel easier to and from San Miguel, which increased business in the area. In 1897, the town celebrated its early history by hosting a centennial of the mission's founding. Parades, dancing, lectures, and concerts were included in the celebration.

In 1928, Mission San Miguel Arcángel was returned to the care of the Franciscan order. The friars began major repairs on the neglected buildings. Today, Franciscans live at the restored mission, which also serves as a parish church, retreat center, and museum. The mission hosts a fiesta on the third Sunday of September each year where visitors can learn more about the mission's history.

On December 22, 2003, a huge earthquake hit San Miguel Arcángel, causing major damage to the church and the surrounding buildings. For years, visitors were not allowed to go inside and see the church's beautiful, original artwork. After a years-long major restoration project, the church was reopened in September 2009. Most of the art was preserved, but more work will be needed to fully restore the many beautiful pieces at San Miguel Arcángel.

The influence of the Spanish missions is still evident in California today. Farming and ranching, two skills brought to the area by the Spanish more than 200 years ago, thrive in California. The state is also a world leader in agricultural production. Mission San Miguel Arcángel stands as a monument, teaching present-day Americans about the lives of the Salinan and the Catholic friars who helped to make California the success it is today.

Today Mission San Miguel is open to the public and serves as a major historical site and tourist destination.

10
Make Your Own Mission Model

To make your own model of the Mission San Miguel Arcángel, you will need:

- pencil
- scissors
- ruler
- Styrofoam
- X-ACTO® knife (ask for an adult's help)
- glue
- Foam Core board
- dried flowers
- corrugated cardboard
- pins
- brown paint
- colored paper
- miniature bell
- moss
- fake plants

DIRECTIONS

Adult supervision is suggested.

Step 1: To make the front and back of the church, cut out two pieces of Styrofoam that are 9" × 12" (22.9 cm × 30.5 cm).

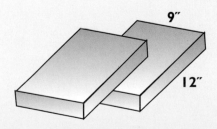

Step 2: Choose one of the pieces to be the front and cut out a door with an X-ACTO knife.

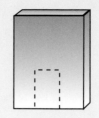

Step 3: Cut two pieces of Styrofoam that are 9" × 12" (22.9 cm × 30.5 cm). These will be the sides of the church.

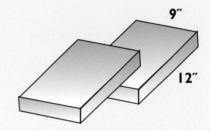

Step 4: Arrange all four pieces in a box shape and glue together. Hold in place for thirty seconds, or until the glue dries.

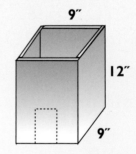

Step 5: Use the large piece of Foam Core board for the base. Attach the church building to the base with glue.

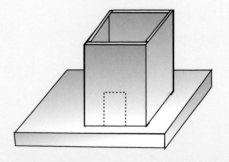

Step 6: Cut out two Styrofoam triangles whose bases are 9" (22.9 cm) long and whose sides are each 6" (15.2 cm). These triangles will be 4" (10.2 cm) high. Glue to the top of the front and back church walls.

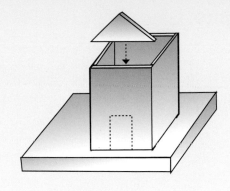

Step 7: To make the arcade, cut two pieces of Styrofoam that are 7" × 3" (17.8 cm × 7.6 cm). These are the front and back pieces.

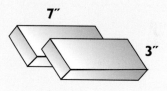

Step 8: Trace two arched doorways in the middle of each Styrofoam arcade wall and cut them out with an X-ACTO knife.

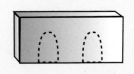

Step 9: To make the arcade roof, cut out a piece of cardboard that is 8" × 5" (20.3 cm × 12.7 cm). Paint the cardboard roof brown. Let paint dry.

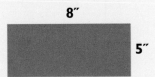

Step 10: Glue the two arcade pieces to the back left side of the church. Then glue the roof to the arcade.

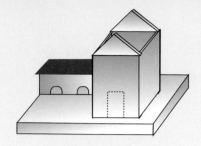

Step 11: To make windows on the church, cut out small squares of cardboard and glue them on the building.

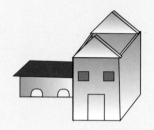

Step 12: Time to decorate! Cut out colored paper in tiny squares and glue them to the floor of the church. Use a round piece of blue paper for an indoor fountain.

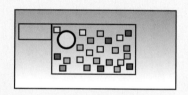

Step 13: Glue a miniature bell in the doorway of the church. Cut paper to make a cross and glue it on the front of the church.

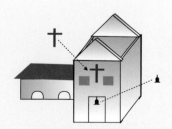

Step 14: Place glue around your mission and arrange moss, dried flowers, or fake plants.

The model of Mission San Miguel Arcángel when completed.

Key Dates in Mission History

1492	Christopher Columbus reaches the West Indies
1542	Cabrillo's expedition to California
1602	Sebastián Vizcaíno sails to California
1713	Fray Junípero Serra is born
1769	Founding of San Diego de Alcalá
1770	Founding of San Carlos Borroméo del Río Carmelo
1771	Founding of San Antonio de Padua and San Gabriel Arcángel
1772	Founding of San Luis Obispo de Tolosa
1775–76	Founding of San Juan Capistrano
1776	Founding of San Francisco de Asís
1776	Declaration of Independence is signed

1777	Founding of Santa Clara de Asís
1782	Founding of San Buenaventura
1784	Fray Serra dies
1786	Founding of Santa Bárbara
1787	Founding of La Purísima Concepción
1791	Founding of Santa Cruz and Nuestra Señora de la Soledad
1797	Founding of San José, San Juan Bautista, San Miguel Arcángel, and San Fernando Rey de España
1798	Founding of San Luis Rey de Francia
1804	Founding of Santa Inés
1817	Founding of San Rafael Arcángel
1823	Founding of San Francisco Solano
1833	Mexico passes Secularization Act
1848	Gold found in northern California
1850	California becomes the thirty-first state

Glossary

adobe (uh-DOH-bee) Sun-dried bricks made of straw, mud, and sometimes manure.

baptism (BAP-tih-zum) A sacrament marked by ritual use of water that makes someone a member of a Christian community and cleanses the person of his or her sins.

Catholicism (kuh-THAH-lih-sih-zum) The faith or practice of Catholic Christianity, which includes following the spiritual leadership of priests headed by the pope.

Christianity (kris-chee-AH-nih-tee) A religion based on the teachings of Jesus Christ and the Bible, practiced by Eastern, Roman Catholic, and Protestant groups.

convert (kun-VURT) To change religious beliefs.

Franciscan (fran-SIS-kin) A member of a Catholic religious group started by Saint Francis of Assisi in 1209.

fresco (FRES-koh) A painting made on wet plaster, which lasts longer than a painting made on a dry wall.

friars (FRY-urz) Brothers in a communal religious order. Friars also can be priests.

indigenous people (in-DIJ-en-us PEA-pel) People native born to a particular region or environment.

neophyte (NEE-oh-fyt) The name for an indigenous person once he or she was baptized into the Christian religion.

restoration (res-tuh-RAY-shun) Working to return something, like a building, to its original state.

sanctuary (SAYNK-choo-weh-ree) The sacred part of a church, which contains the altar.

secularization (seh-kyoo-lur-ih-ZAY-shun) A process by which the mission lands were made to be nonreligious.

viceroy (VYS-roy) A government official who rules an area as a representative of the king.

Pronunciation Guide

alcaldes (ahl-KAHL-des)

atole (ah-TOH-lay)

convento (kom-BEN-toh)

fiestas (fee-EHS-tahs)

fray (FRAY)

monjerío (mohn-hay-REE-oh)

pozole (poh-SOH-lay)

ranchería (rahn-cheh-REE-ah)

ranchos (RAHN-chohs)

siesta (see-EHS-tah)

vaqueros (bah-KEH-rohs)

Find Out More

To learn more about the California missions, check out these books and websites.

BOOKS

Bellezza, Robert A. *Missions of Central California.* Charleston, SC: Arcadia Publishing, 2013.

Brower, Pauline. *Inland Valleys: Missions of California.* Minneapolis, MN: Lerner Publishing, 2008.

Price, Sean. *The Birth of a State: California Missions.* Chicago, IL: Raintree, 2008.

Young, Stanley. *The Missions of California.* San Francisco, CA: Chronicle Books, 2004.

WEBSITES

California Missions Resource Center

www.missionscalifornia.com

This is a resource for facts on all of the California Missions.

California Mission Studies Association

www.californiamissionstudies.com

This is a great source for summaries of the California Missions.

San Diego History Center

www.sandiegohistory.org/journal/69fall/struggle.htm

This website is part of the San Diego history center. It provides articles from its magazine, *The Journal of San Diego History*, including articles about the Missions.

Index